*New Englanders in
Nova Albion*

A GALLERY OF NEW ENGLAND VISITORS

New Englanders in Nova Albion:
Some 19th Century Views
of California

by JAMES D. HART

Delivered on the occasion of the
third annual Bromsen lecture
May 3, 1975

BOSTON

Trustees of the Public Library of the City of Boston

1976

Maury A. Bromsen Lecture
in Humanistic Bibliography, No. 3

Library of Congress Cataloging in Publication Data
Hart, James David, 1911–
  New Englanders in Nova Albion.

  (Maury A. Bromsen lecture in humanistic bibliography; no. 3)
  1. California—Discovery and exploration—Addresses, essays, lectures. 2. New Englanders in California—Addresses, essays, lectures.   I. Title.   II. Series.
F864.H317   917.94′04   76-52
ISBN 0-89073-008-3

Copyright © 1976 by Trustees of the Public Library
of the City of Boston

Foreword

The Boston Public Library is pleased to present in book form the third annual Maury A. Bromsen Lecture in Humanistic Bibliography. Mr. Bromsen, bookman and scholar in the field of bibliography and the history of the Americas, had endowed this lectureship in memory of his mother, Rose Eisenberg Bromsen (1885–1968).

It is most appropriate for the year in which Boston celebrates the opening of the Bicentennial that the Bromsen Lecture Committee select as the lecturer a distinguished authority in American literature and historical bibliography. In "New Englanders in Nova Albion: Some 19th Century Views of California" Dr. James D. Hart provides "documentation for a small but special sort of cultural history." This skillfully woven account of New England visitors' writings on their westward explorations and discoveries enriches one's understanding of the growth of our country and invites consideration of other special facets of our history.

Dr. Hart has been director of The Bancroft Library of the University of California, Berkeley, since 1970, an institution whose scope has been expanded from rare books and manuscripts of the American West and Latin America to include all special collections. As author, teacher, editor, librarian, bibliophile, and printer, Mr. Hart has made significant contributions to the fields of American literature and history. His *Oxford Companion to American Literature* is a standard reference work. The edited works of Richard Henry Dana, Francis Parkman, Robert Louis Stevenson, and Frank Norris and *American Images of Spanish California* have been important contributions to the literature of the American West. We are pleased to add this publication to the list.

PHILIP J. McNIFF
DIRECTOR AND LIBRARIAN

For Ruth, again and always

New Englanders in Nova Albion: Some 19th Century Views of California

RIGHT FROM the beginning the first settlers of America were conscious of the West. Their westernmost goal was only just beyond the fringe of land fronting the Atlantic, yet they had a sense that the earth stretching all the way to the Pacific belonged to them. Once they had tamed their first frontier and converted or driven out its brutish Indians, they were prepared to occupy lands farther west. This was what King Charles promised the Governor and the Company of Massachusetts Bay when his royal patent of 1628/9 conferred on them "the maine landes from Sea to Sea," in a magnificent gift of all fields and woods, all rivers and lakes from eastern to western coasts. Even as they prepared to make their first landings on American soil the English considered that they had a divinely appointed mission to possess its entire wilderness. So it was that John Winthrop, on the eve of leaving England to become a colonist in 1630, argued that the Indians must give way to the whites, for "the whole earth is the Lord's garden, and he hath given it to the sons of Adam to be tilled and improved by them." In the minds of Winthrop and his colleagues, the legitimate sons of Adam were English-speaking Puritans, the only proper heirs of the Lord's land from sea to shining sea.

A half century before Englishmen like Winthrop colonized the western seaboard of the Atlantic and designated their scattered settlements as New England, Sir Francis Drake had marked out a Nova Albion on the Pacific end of the American continent. Three thousand miles separated these twin names on the land but it was tacitly understood that they were to be joined by Englishmen or, as was later conceived, by their successors called Americans. Long before the tremendous difficulty of a transcontinental passage was much thought of or clearly recognized, its eventual accomplishment was accepted as inevitable. In terms of physiography, words on charters or maps were meaningless beside the realities of mountains, plains, deserts, and rivers, but in terms of psychology they were significant as an earnest of exploration and settlement, a call to the pioneer who would make the word become deed.

On this centuries-long road across the continent men were animated by various pressures, some emotional, some practical. Their urges were often almost inextricably tangled. As frontiers were pushed away from seaboard settlements, the pioneers were sometimes consciously, mostly unwittingly, moving toward the distant and fabled shores of the Pacific. California, first named in a 16th-century Spanish romance as an island "very near the Terrestrial Paradise," did not come into the New Englanders' consciousness for a long time, but in geographic fact and mythic fancy it was the ultimate western region toward which they hankered, even though they knew neither its Spanish designation nor the Latin one of Nova Albion that had been applied by Drake.

The New Englanders' move west was not a direct drift for they had their hands more than full in the explorations, battles, and settlements that led them north and south along their Atlantic seaboard. Far, far off lay the old, rich, and fabulous outposts of the Spanish empire that resisted all intrusions, despite Drake's foray. There was a French empire nearer at hand to fight during the 18th century and the barriers of the Alleghenies were enough mountains to cope with for a long time. The wilderness of what we now consider the nearer Middle West, terminating in New Spain's Mississippi River border, seemed distant enough for 18th-century colonists from New England. So it was not by land that the New Englanders moved toward the remote and fabulous realm of California but rather it came within their purview as their fisheries, fur business, and shipping interests led them around Cape Horn and up into the Pacific Ocean pursuing whales and sea otters, and later to bargain for beaver and cow hides that could be got in trade with the local population.

In 1792 Robert Gray, of Rhode Island and Boston, took his merchant ship *Columbia* into the Pacific Northwest region above the Spanish possessions and up the river that came to be named for his vessel. Simultaneously Boston schooners began to venture into the China trade and picked up exotic sandalwood in the islands now named Hawaiian. But California's coast was prohibited to strangers and landings were illegal all during the 18th century and into the early 19th. Nevertheless, a few daring New Englanders put in at Monterey or San Diego under the pretext or actual need of wood and water but they were forced out quickly. So by 1800 California's primitive ports had been visited by very few foreigners, yet those who had seen them had such good Yankee names as Captain Ebenezer Dorr and Captain Charles Winship who came aboard ships titled the *Eliza* and the *Betsey*.

The first printed report about California by a New Englander was written by William Shaler, a Connecticut sea captain, who from 1803 to 1805 illegally collected sea otter pelts in California's ports and took them to market in China.

In 1808 he published his account in the *American Register*, a semiannual almanac on matters of interest to the nascent United States. Shaler's text set the tone for a long series of Yankee observations on this Latin land. The natural scene he praised for its agreeable climate, terrain, and flora, declaring that "the country is remarkably fine, well-watered, and covered with forests," and observed that even the time of year that is harsh in New England was friendly here for "in the winter season, the bays and harbours of California abound with geese, brant, duck, etc." And so Shaler was the first of many New Englanders to cast an openly appreciative and a tacitly covetous eye on the Nova Albion that Drake too had wanted to possess three hundred and twenty-five years earlier. Shaler called the region "An object worthy the attention of the great maritime powers," and then concluded, "the conquest of this country would be absolutely nothing; it would fall without an effort to the most inconsiderable force." The Mexicans, suspecting and fearing just such sentiments, hustled Shaler and all other foreigners out of their ports as fast as they possibly could.

But there was no stopping the Yankees. Before long another New Englander not only illegally visited a California port but actually decided to make his home in the country, though with no such grand design as that envisioned by Shaler. He was just a common Boston sailor in his twenties named Thomas Doak who deserted from the *Albatross* in 1816 and became the first American citizen to settle permanently in California. Naturally this required his conversion to Catholicism and his allegiance to a foreign power. So plain Thomas became Felipe Santiago and under that lush cognomen married an heiress of the Castro family, one of the great rancheros of the region. Doak gave up his New England heritage only in order to enjoy life in California but soon enough there were other, more important men from Massachusetts who dreamed of settling in California as representatives of their own culture. So it was that the bicentennial of the *Mayflower* landing caused Daniel Webster to declare in his orotund way: "Ere long the sons of the Pilgrims will be on the shores of the Pacific."

Webster's literal vision, though not his desire, soon came true. Less than ten years after Doak jumped ship another New Englander also became a California settler but in a more seemly style. He was William Goodwin Dana, a member of a near-Brahmin family with 17th-century roots in the old Bay Colony. He came to California as master of a trading vessel in 1825 and then decided to remain. To do so he too of course had to be naturalized and that meant that first he had to be converted to Catholicism. But as a more famous relative of his later said, he was only one of many Calvinists "who left their conscience at Cape Horn." Don Guillermo Dana seems to have had no qualms about his change of faith and nationality for he settled down as a happy, blond ranchero north of Santa Barbara with his wife, a member of the great Carrillo family, and became a popular grandee of the area.

A few years later he was coincidentally followed by a remote relative, Richard Henry Dana, Jr., the best known of all New England visitors to California. The two Danas never met for the families seemed to have been estranged (presumably because of Guillermo's apostasy) and the lesser but earlier traveler to California is never mentioned by the later in the account of his voyage, which is also the most important literary statement of a New Englander's view of California life and culture under Mexican rule.

The settled, substantial Guillermo was approaching forty when his teen-aged relative put in to California as a common sailor aboard the hide-trading brig *Pilgrim*. The voyage of just four months from Boston to Santa Barbara had changed him, as he later recalled, from a boy accustomed to be garbed in "the tight frock-coat, silk cap and kid gloves of an undergraduate at Harvard, to the loose duck trousers, checked shirt and tarpaulin hat of a sailor." By the time he reached California Dana had left not his conscience but his life as a young gentleman behind him. He left behind too the sickliness that came from a case of measles which had so weakened his eyesight that he could not keep up with his Harvard class and that led him to seek a cure for it, as he said, "by an entire change of life, and by a long absence from books, with plenty of hard work, plain food, and open air." These he got in full measure so that he was in good health and able to share in the new experiences that came his way. Shipboard experience first cured his eyes and then opened them to new ways of life.

What he saw he saw clearly in terms of scene and situation for his experiences at sea had knocked out most of the romanticism that he had savored as a cultivated young Cantabrigian. But his vision was still affected by his family heritage and by his regional attitudes and principles. He never became, as he feared he might, a "sailor in every respect, mind and habits, as well as body, *nolens volens*." Always deep within him, he knew that he was a Dana, a member of a family two hundred years settled in Massachusetts, and, as he was to say, hopeful that there would "always be a Richard Henry Dana to stand before the Lord." He served the Lord in his inherited style as a Calvinist and a Congregationalist who believed that certain people are elect but that all people—elect or not—should preserve their precious time and use it for good purposes. Accordingly his high principles sometimes came close to being toplofty as he surveyed the new situations to which life aboard ship brought him. He sympathized with other sailors and when he saw them grievously mistreated he determined to speak out on their behalf, but though he sympathetically declared that their lives were "at best a mixture of a little good with much evil, and a little pleasure with much pain," he looked upon his fellows in the forecastle with an attitude of *noblesse oblige* and described them as "that class of beings with whom my lot had so long been cast."

The experiences that Dana underwent in the two years roughly bounded by his nineteenth and his twentieth birthdays formed the basis for his personal narrative, *Two Years Before the Mast*. He prohibited its publishers from placing his name on the title page because as a gentleman it was not seemly to expose one's personal experiences, but the authorship was soon widely known for the narrative became enormously popular. It was read for several reasons, not only as a presentation of one young man's experiences but also as a revelation of life in the American merchant marine that was at just that moment coming to its peak, sailing all the waters of the world and finally challenging British supremacy of the seas. Here, at last, was a book that truly told what the life of a common sailor was like for, as Dana said, his intention was not to talk about " 'blue water,' 'blue jackets,' 'open hearts,' 'seeing God's hand on the deep,' and so forth" but to "take this up like any other practical subject," treating "sailors as they are—men to be fed, and clothed, and lodged, for whom laws must be made and executed, and who are to be instructed in useful knowledge, and above all to be brought under religious influence and restraint." It was this realistic, although also pious purpose that animated Dana's book and that delighted a polite public who had too long been given a speciously sentimental sense of life at sea as they were told of it only by captains or proper passengers.

Two Years Before the Mast represented a new way of depicting life at sea and yet the title was somewhat inaccurate because for all but nine months Dana focused as much or more upon the land as upon the sea. He took about four months to sail from Boston to the west coast and about as long to return, but all the rest of the time was spent either ashore or coasting up and down among the harbors of California. In keeping with the diary-like form of the narrative, the first eight chapters deal with the voyage outward bound and the last six with the trip home, but they simply frame the larger, central segment of twenty-one chapters. It is these core chapters that concentrate upon Dana's view of California as it was during the era of Mexican dominion.

From January 1835 to early May of the next year Dana was never farther at sea than a few miles off California's shore and most of his time he spent in its ports and pueblos. Naturally Dana did not get to the interior, but then there was very little population away from the coast and he saw something of all the seaboard settlements. Yet no matter how long he stayed ashore Dana was always just a common sailor attached to a vessel whose captain happily admitted that he was "a slave driver,— a nigger driver," and whom Dana declared was the type to "call a sailor 'a son of a bitch,' and knock him down with a handspike." Such a person was not about to let one of his crew become a casual sightseer of life in a foreign land.

Nevertheless, Dana had a far better opportunity than his fellows to see life ashore. The captain and the company's local agent were aware that he came of a prominent and influential family, a force that in time helped him transfer from the harsh discipline of Captain Frank Thompson's brig to the more equitable ship *Alert*. Both officers recognized him as an educated man whose Greek and Latin had been supplemented by the more useful Spanish he worked up on the voyage so that he was sent "for provisions, or to take letters and messages," and generally served as an informal liaison between ship and shore. Thus Dana put in a lot of time in the ports and the country around them and with a typical expression of his New England conscience he castigated the way in which other sailors would "misspend" their similar but shorter leaves by flirting with girls and drinking in *pulperias* while he used his time to make tours on horseback, to visit nearby missions, and in general obtain an understanding of what he called "the character and habits of the people, as well as the institutions under which they lived."

The result of this observation he later spread over some three hundred pages of his account, enough to make a book in itself. Just as Dana declared that he had been put in a position to "learn truths by strong contrasts," in juxtaposing his former life with that of the forecastle, so he found lessons by explicitly or tacitly contrasting the relaxed Latin ways of the Californios with the Protestant ethic of his native New England. Without question the Latins were charming for they possessed a grace of movement, a softness of speech, and an attractively easy-going attitude toward life, but they offended Dana's ingrained ethic because, as he declared, they lacked "industry, frugality, and enterprise." Much as he found some of their style of life appealing, he self-righteously concluded: "There are no people to whom the newly invented Yankee word 'loafer' is more applicable than to the Spanish Americans." His conclusions were based not only upon views of the ordinary people but, at a little further remove, of the behavior of the local aristocrats. His best sight of them came when Doña Anita de la Guerra, the youngest daughter of Santa Barbara's leading grandee, was married to Alfred Robinson, the agent of the company to which Dana's ships belonged. From an outer circle he was able to watch the dance in her father's courtyard that celebrated the wedding. There he observed young Don Juan Bandini, the extravagant heir of one of the finer families, who, though Dana declared his poverty, was known even to "half-naked Indian boys of the street," was gorgeously arrayed in "white pantaloons, neatly made, a short jacket of dark silk, gaily figured, white stockings and thin morocco slippers upon his very small feet" as he danced "with the grace and daintiness of a young fawn," a striking contrast to the angular awkwardness of the groom, a New England businessman rigged out in "a tight black swallow-tailed coat just imported from Boston, a high stiff cravat, looking," as Dana said, "as if he had been pinned and skewered, with only his feet and hands left free."

In an occasional observation like this Dana recognizes some superior qualities in the California way of life but generally its people, their values, and their behavior are captiously considered from the supercilious vantage point of a New Englander. But no matter how critical he is, Dana is remarkably unemotional and his comments are made in clear and vivid statements, in keeping with the tenets of composition and rhetoric taught at Harvard by Professor Edward Tyrrell Channing, the mentor not only of Dana but of Emerson, Oliver Wendell Holmes, and many another New England spokesman. Generally spare in statement and always precise in style, Dana as a son of New England in an alien land was chary of romantic speculation, sweeping philosophic commentary, and even generalized statements. He placed his emphasis upon that which he could see directly before him so that what he observed could be described cogently and clearly. His clarity of view is sustained by a precision in English so fine that, amusingly enough, a passage from his autobiographical text and one from Benjamin Franklin, another son of New England, have come to be used by American optometrists as standard eye tests so that their patients will have exact and simple diction with which to cope.

Dana's description is built upon one particular after the other. The piece of land or sea directly before him is his explicit concern, not a broad romantic landscape. He refers always to the specific and builds his description on the basis of particulars. The reader is given on the printed page almost exactly what the author obtained in his original experience. One sees, bit by bit, what Dana saw, and in the sequence of his own viewing. Always his narrative is built on precise perception and exact statement, not on generalization nor heightened rhetoric. Even when he treats a large landscape and concludes with a broad statement, Dana works in just this way. So it is that he creates a grand description of San Francisco Bay, proceeding with great exactitude from one particular fragment to another to achieve the sense of panorama:

We sailed down this magnificent bay with a light wind, the tide, which was running out, carrying us at the rate of four or five knots. It was a fine day; the first of entire sunshine we had had for more than a month. We passed directly under the high cliff on which the presidio is built, and stood into the middle of the bay, from whence we could see small bays making up into the interior, large and beautifully wooded islands, and the mouths of several rivers. If California ever becomes a prosperous country, this bay will be the centre of its prosperity. The abundance of wood and water; the extreme fertility of its shores; the excellence of its climate, which is as near to being perfect as any in the world; and its facilities for navigation, affording the best anchoring-grounds in the whole western coast of America—all fit it for a place of great importance.

Here is what might for Dana be called a spacious passage. It consists of 159 words, nearly every one of them Anglo-Saxon in origin. Of those 159 words only 12 are of two syllables. Only 10 are of three syllables, and they are all simple words: anchoring, importance, excellence. Leaving aside proper names, only 6 of the words are of four syllables, and every one of those is a common word: magnificent, beautifully, prosperity, fertility, facilities, navigation. And one should observe that the longer words do not come until the end of the passage, just as the larger view of the Bay does not come until Dana has proceeded, point by point, spot by spot, to describe what lies directly before him, moment after moment. Moreover, he does not come to any generalities until he has given us every detail of the water (the tide running out), of the rate of progress (four or five knots), and the climate (the first sunshine for more than a month). Dana's adjectives are few and most commonly define matters of size, shape, color, or other verifiable facts. He generally does not use adjectives for emotion or aesthetic effect alone. He creates a tableau but does it with a style that is the quintessence of the laconic Yankee. This was Dana's way of working in his book so that although he creates the sense of an alien culture his observations are commonly directed toward particular situations or specific scenes that ultimately create a totality of effect. In these ways *Two Years Before the Mast* became the major statement of a New Englander's view of California.

Both before and after Dana's year and a half on the coast, other sailors put into California's harbors to carry on the great trade of hide droghing. Local cowhides were collected as fast as the Mexicans could provide them, shipped back in the holds of Bryant, Sturgis and Company vessels to be made into shoes at Lynn, Massachusetts, and some of the finished products brought back to California a year or so later to be sold for cash or traded for more of the raw hides of which they were made. The firm of Bryant, Sturgis not only combined shipping and trading so effectively that it needed a resident manager like Alfred Robinson but it was so monopolistic that before long the Californios came to use the name Boston as synonymous with the United States.

Even though the Californios considered the hide droghers' home port and the whole nation to which it belonged to be one and the same, they were not the only kind of Yankee traders to seep into and to stay in California. There was, for example, Abel Stearns of Massachusetts who lived in Mexico for three years before emigrating to Los Angeles in 1829 to become its leading merchant. There he married into the distinguished Bandini family (Don Juan became his father-in-law) and became the largest landowner and cattle raiser in southern California and an official of its Mexican government. And then there was Nathan Spear, whose trading took him to the South Seas and the Sandwich Islands before he reached Monterey in 1831 and moved on to become one of the first residents of Yerba Buena. Off the waterfront of this ur–San Francisco settlement lay an island he took over to pasture his goats, thus for a long time providing the name Goat Island to the land that now serves as the pivotal point in the long San Francisco–Oakland Bay Bridge. Spears' nephew, William Heath Davis, was a more exotic specimen of a Californian with a Boston background. His father was a shipmaster hailing from Massachusetts but his mother was a Polynesian from Hawaii. Davis was brought to California as a youngster several times on his father's trading expeditions before he settled down there in 1838, aged sixteen. The most striking of all the Yankees in California was Thomas Oliver Larkin of Charlestown, Massachusetts, who sailed as a bachelor in his late twenties to California in 1831 and not long after arrival the following April became a married man by wedding a widow, Rachel Hobson Holmes, whom he had met on shipboard. Their son became the first child of United States parents born in California. Larkin himself not only managed to make a fortune through a store and through trade with Mexico and the Sandwich Islands but he avoided becoming a Mexican citizen and quietly supported Alvarado's revolution of 1836 for a free and sovereign California. Larkin's greatest distinction lay in his service as the first and only consul of the United States to California, a post he held from 1844 until the conquest of the Mexican War no longer made it necessary. In this capacity he not only looked after American interests and aided distressed United States seamen but, in keeping with his stance toward Alvarado, he indicated that he would be sympathetic to a California that asserted its independence from Mexico and acted in accordance with Secretary of State Buchanan's secret message that "Whilst the President will make no effort and use no influence to induce California to become one of the free and independent States of this Union, yet if the People should desire to unite their destiny with ours, they would be received as brethren, whenever this can be done, without affording Mexico just cause of complaint."

Larkin was involved in a ticklish business, in part because there were increasing numbers of New Englanders and other American-born men who had become subjects of Mexico allied by marriage with the leading local Mexican or Spanish families. Important among these was Alfred Robinson, the resident manager of the shipping firm for which Dana had worked in the lowest capacity. By the wedding that Dana had peeked at, the Bostonian had become affiliated with the local aristocracy, given up his Protestant status as what the local clergy described as an "unbaptized person," and taken on the new names of José María Alfredo Robinson. Over the years he and Doña Anita lived by turns in the eastern United States and in California, as his business required. These different residences were representative of the divergent points of view he came to express in his book that was well known after 1846 under the title *Life in California*. Having married into the higher society of the Californios, Robinson obviously wanted to depict these people in a more favorable light than that in which they were displayed in the best-selling book by the one-time common sailor Dana. Although he admits to the indolence of the Mexican men of California, he praises the ladies for their "chastity, industrious habits, and correct deportment." At the same time that he is eager to see the American "banner of liberty" planted "at the entrance of the noble, the spacious bay of San Francisco," he shows sympathy toward some of the Spanish ways of life and for the Californio's religion that became his own. Nevertheless, in personal letters to his brother in-law Pablo he equates civilization with the United States and in 1846 contends that "California has now begun to exist!" only with the coming of Americans. Robinson finally reaches the view: "There is nothing like the mixture of blood. The Yankee and Spanish blood produce good soldiers," he declared during an international incident in 1854, linking the two cultures that he shared. Thus the erstwhile New Englander Robinson was led by his personal situation to present a more balanced treatment of California than that which Dana had popularized a few years earlier.

Still another person who was part of the great Bryant, Sturgis enterprise provided a further Yankee view of California. He was William Henry Thomes, a Down East Maine boy bred in Boston, whose association with the Company was on just the same low level as Dana's. Indeed, the teen-aged Thomes, who arrived in California in 1843, three years after Dana's narrative was published, at one time said that his voyage was influenced by the romance and adventure of that book, and at another time that he too was troubled by bad eyesight and determined to cure it in the same way. The different explanations are typical of Thomes for he was more a romancer than a reporter. Besides, he did not write about California until forty years after the events he experienced there. The recollections of a sixty-year-old man were further adulterated because in his maturity he had become a professional writer of adventure tales for boys and had doubtless been influenced by some other authors' fiction about the Spanish California that was gone. Nevertheless, during his residence there the eighteen-year-old Thomes saw and did many of the same things as Dana because their situations were similar and he was admittedly influenced by the earlier writer. But Thomes was not only easy-going by temperament, he was also a yarn spinner for young people by profession so his two books do not attempt the same sort of sober, even sociological interpretation that is found in *Two Years Before the Mast*. The best of Thomes' works is his autobiographical narrative, *On Land and Sea*, for its sequel, *Lewey and I*, is frankly a fictive rendering of what happened to him and a friend after they jumped ship and got involved in the Bear Flag War. Even the ostensibly factual book and his *Recollections* prepared for Hubert Howe Bancroft move much like an adventure story and lack the careful modeling of Dana's more sober and interpretative treatment.

So simple a matter as the descriptions by Dana and Thomes of their first views of Monterey points up the differences between the men and their writings. Dana through sharp visual images sets forth in clear simple diction the exact appearance of the place, point by point, as he looks upon it: "the pretty lawn on which it stands, as green as sun and rain could make it; the pine wood on the south; the small river on the north side; the adobe houses, with their white walls and red-tiled roofs, dotted about on the green; the low, white presidio, with its soiled tricolored flag flying, and the discordant din of drums and trumpets of the noon parade." Thomes lacking both the nice eye and ear of Dana just says that Monterey had "houses all of adobe scattered and dropped around in various places without regard to location or situation as though some crazy man had planned and built the town." But, writing forty years after the conquest, Thomes did sentimentalize the past and treat Mexican California with a romance shunned by the harder-headed contemporary view of Dana. So it was that Thomes wrote of Santa Barbara:

There we saw the pleasantest happiest quietest handsomest little place that we had seen on the Coast, with the most beautiful girls and the most courteous and able Spanish Mexican gentlemen, and some of the oldest families resided there. Their wealth was enormous in cattle and lands. . . . The occupation of the ladies in Santa Barbara was the same as in Monterey, going to Mass and confessions, singing and dancing, embroideries, and eating and sleeping, and a more happy and contented set of mortals seem never to have existed on the face of the Earth than those Spanish Mexican families. . . . The people of the present day have but little idea of the grandeur of the old Spanish Mexican families, of their generous hospitality, of the number of retainers that each family possessed and the little trouble which they took to entertain you, yet of the hearty manner in which they received you and the fervent manner in which they bid you "God speed" on your journey and to come again when you were disposed, though if you remained with them a week, a month or six months and had offered to recompense them for their trouble, it would have been looked upon as an insult almost unpardonable. . . . Such was life in California in those early days, a simple Arcadian sort of life with a happy, contented people who were rich in lands and cattle, cared nothing for wealth, firm in their friendships bitter and deadly in their hostilities, not always truthful and the lower class not always honest, but the upper classes gentlemanly, polished with a natural born courtesy that seemed to be innate. On the whole you could not help liking them in spite of their procrastinations and as for the women, it was utterly impossible for a susceptible American to be in their society without loving them and you can hardly blame them that to obtain possession they would renounce their own religion and embrace Catholicism.

A more mature and responsible view of California by an older New Englander came from the Reverend Walter Colton. His father had served for fifty years as a deacon of a Congregational church in Rutland County, Vermont, and his mother, whose given name was Thankful, had also reared him in the old Puritan traditions. After education at Yale he himself was ordained in the ministry, but in 1830, age thirty-three, poor health caused him, like Dana, to go to sea to be cured by what he hoped would be a wholesome way of life. The nautical experience he chose was one specially suited to his maturity and experience for he enlisted as a chaplain in the United States Navy. His first voyage took him to Lisbon, Gibralter, Smyrna, Constantinople, and Athens. After stints ashore that included some editorial work and the writing of books of impressions about his travels, he remained with the Navy which again ordered him to sea in late 1845. His ship, bound for Pacific waters, arrived in California just a moment after the Bear Flag War broke out and Colton was soon involved in the last days of the Mexican Republic and its conquest by the United States. As soon as the battle was won Commodore Stockton, the American military governor, named Colton alcalde, or mayor of Monterey. In this capacity Colton became a leader of American California, founding its first newspaper and sponsoring a public school. All told, he spent three significant years in California, arriving when it was still Mexican, leaving when it was on the eve of statehood. When Colton stepped ashore the population was about ten thousand; when he left, it had ballooned to two hundred thousand. It was of the earlier, quiet California that he wrote most warmly in his diary-like book, *Three Years in California*, first published in 1850. Despite his sturdy New England background, there is almost nothing of the view of upstage Protestantism in his account for he appreciated the Californios and their ways of life tremendously. Thus he wrote:

> There are no people that I have ever been among who enjoy life so thoroughly as the Californians. Their habits are simple; their wants few; nature rolls almost every thing spontaneously into their lap. Their cattle, horses, and sheep roam at large—not a

blade of grass is cut, and none is required. The harvest waves wherever the plough and harrow have been; and the grain which the wind scatters this year, serves as seed for the next. The slight labor required is more a diversion than a toil; and even this is shared by the Indian. They attach no value to money, except as it administers to their pleasures. A fortune, without the facilities of enjoying it, is with them no object of emulation or envy. Their happiness flows from a fount that has very little connection with their outward circumstances.

There is hardly a shanty among them which does not contain more true contentment, more genuine gladness of the heart, than you will meet with in the most princely palace. Their hospitality knows no bounds; they are always glad to see you, come when you may; take a pleasure in entertaining you while you remain; and only regret that your business calls you away. If you are sick, there is nothing which sympathy and care can devise or perform which is not done for you. No sister ever hung over the throbbing brain or fluttering pulse of a brother with more tenderness and fidelity. This is as true of the lady whose hand has only figured her embroidery or swept her guitar, as of the cottage-girl wringing from her laundry the foam of the mountain stream; and all this from the *heart*!

Colton was entranced and yet somewhat amused by the people into whose lives he had been thrust. He found them so romantic, so different from the New Englanders to whom he was accustomed, that he wrote of them like an anthropologist surveying an alien tribe. Thus, early on in his book he gives a view of the male of the species:

A Californian is most at home in his saddle; there he has some claims to originality, if not in character then in costume. His hat, with its conical crown and broad rim, throws back the sun's rays from its dark, glazed surface. It is fastened on by a band which passes under his chin, and rests on a red handkerchief, which turbans his head, from beneath which his black locks flow out upon the wind.

The collar of his linen rolls over that of his blue spencer, which is open under the chin, is fitted closely to his waist, and often ornamented with double rows of buttons and silk braid. His trowsers, which are fastened around his loins by a red sash, are open to the knee, to which his buckskin leggins ascend over his white cotton drawers. His buckskin shoes are armed with heavy spurs, which have a shaft some ten inches long, at the end of which is a roller, which bristles out into six points, three inches long, against which steel plates rattle with a quick, sharp sound.

His feet rest in stirrups of wood, carved from the solid oak, and which are extremely strong and heavy. His saddle rises high fore and aft, and is broadly skirted with leather, which is stamped into figures, through the interstices of which red and green silk flash out with gay effect. The reins of his bridle are thick and narrow, and the headstall is profusely ornamented with silver plate. His horse, with his long flowing mane, arching neck, broad chest, full flanks, and slender legs, is full of fire. He seldom trots, and will gallop all day without seeming to be weary. On his back is the Californian's home. Leave him this home, and you may have the rest of the world.

Yet for all his delight with the equestrian Californians, Colton was bemused by these men's behavior and temperament. As illustration he wrote:

Our bay is full of the finest fish, and yet it is rare to meet one on the table. There is not a boat here in which one can safely trust himself a cable's length from land. And if there were, there would be no Californians to row it. Could they go to sea on their horses, and fish from their saddles, they would often be seen dashing through the surf; but to sit quietly in a boat and bob a line, is entirely too tame a business. Put a fish on land, and give him the speed of the buck, and he would have a dozen Californians and forty hounds on his trail.

The Californio's dedication to riding and sporting he found quaint and rather charming but as a Protestant divine Colton did have some strictures, though they were pretty light, about the behavior of the native Catholics. Near the beginning of his book he observed:

Till the Americans took possession of Monterey, the Sabbath was devoted to amusement. The Indians gave themselves up to liquor, the Mexicans and Californians to dancing. Whether the bottle or the fiddle had the most votaries it would be difficult to say.

But despite their failings he obviously appreciated the dispositions and style of life of the native Californians when contrasted to the greedy citizens of his own country who rushed pell-mell into California upon the discovery of gold and grubbed through its land, bringing disorder and destruction. Sadly he wrote toward the end of his book: "If I must be cast in sickness or destitution on the care of the stranger, let it be in California; but let it be before American avarice has hardened the heart and made a god of gold."

Colton's final reflections are like those of Thomes who also emphasized his appreciation of the Californios by contrasting them with the invaders from the United States. "I need not say," Thomes declared, "that the coming of the Americans when the news of the gold discovery was carried to the East changed all . . . , and from being an affectionate, confiding people, they became a suspicious, jealous and discontented race."

Nevertheless, Thomes took off for California a second time during the gold rush that attracted great numbers of men from all of the United States, New England included. As a pioneer of the early 1840's he thought he knew his way around well enough to make a fortune in the land where he had once lived. So in January 1849 he paid $300 to buy a share in the Boston and California Joint Stock Mining and Trading Company which entitled him to sail on the good ship *Edward Everett*. The one-time Governor of Massachusetts, now risen to the higher post of President of Harvard

College, interested himself in the voyagers who were to sail on the bark named for him. To each of the one hundred incipient miners he gave a copy of the Scriptures with these words: "You are going to a strange country. Take the Bible in one hand and your New England civilization in the other, and make your mark upon the people and the country." And thus equipped the first of the one hundred twenty-four New England companies organized to mine gold set sail for California.

By the time Thomes and his fellows got to the Mother Lode they had shed a lot of New England civilization and their right hand, like their left, was busy with a pan to sift gold from the rivers and streams of California. Indeed, Thomes comments that the day before he left Benicia for the mines he saw a large number of the famous Everett Bibles lying on the counter in a saloon where the bartender had taken them in trade, first at fifty cents apiece, then, when they got too numerous, for a quarter.

Like plenty of other '49'ers, whether bred in New England or not, Thomes found little gold and what he got was often stolen by others. No wonder that he later placed a fictive character in a comparable situation and had him say, "It's precious little fun I've seen in that country." So in 1851 he sailed from California, first to Hawaii, where he stayed for some months and got material for an adventurous book, then on to Australia, whose gold mines provided background for still another boys' story, and finally home, to find success at last as a popular writer. Though his second experience in California was unsatisfactory, Thomes came back once again, this time in the 1880's, to glory in the official status of an early argonaut, now grown portly and pompous. In his latest incarnation he not only dictated his memoirs for Hubert Howe Bancroft, the leading local historian, but founded the parochially pious Society of California Pioneers.

During the 1840's and '50's a lot of other New Englanders were also becoming eligible for membership in the Society of California Pioneers by making their way west. They were not nearly so numerous as those who came from other parts of the United States yet, as the proper Bostonian Francis Parkman said of the emigrants he met on the Oregon Trail in 1846, "New England sends but a small proportion but they are better furnished than the rest." Of the rest he said simply that they were "totally devoid of any sense of delicacy or propriety." And William Lewis Manly, in considering some of his fellow travelers of 1849, simply noted, "Really, my New England ideas . . . were somewhat shocked."

As these voyagers might have expected, one of the very finest commentators on the gold rush scene was a New Englander. More than that, she was a lady. She was christened Louise Amelia Knapp Smith in New Jersey in 1819, for that is where her father, a Williams College alumnus, was temporarily headmaster of a private school. But she was soon back on her ancestral heath of Amherst to be educated first at the Female Seminary of Charlestown, in the purlieus of Boston, and then at the Amherst Academy where Emily Dickinson was also a student. She had a proper romance with Alexander Hill Everett, brother of the doughty Edward Everett, but she married a young doctor, Fayette Clapp, from a town near Amherst, and with him she sailed to California in the golden year of 1849. While he practiced his profession at Rich Bar and other jerry-built Feather River mining settlements, she entertained herself and her sister Mary Jane, at home in Massachusetts, by writing a series of witty letters describing her new surroundings. She signed them by the unexplained pseudonym Dame Shirley and perhaps really mailed them to the sister she called Molly, but before long she put them into print in a California literary journal properly titled the *Pioneer*.

The twenty-three Shirley letters are a curious combination of clear, witty observation and literary self-consciousness. In an arch way she likens herself to Lady Mary Wortley Montagu and Mme de Sévigné and with some self-consciousness strives for "fine" writing, the sort of specious literary elegance that she may have been taught at Amherst Academy and that she presumably affected later when she became a schoolteacher. So it is that she doesn't see a deer, she "descries" it; she isn't housed, she is "ensconced"; and she shows herself to be a cultivated lady by quoting from the Bible, Bunyan, Shakespeare, and Tennyson.

Apparently Shirley's favorite author was Dickens for she cites or quotes him more frequently than any other and his writings obviously influenced her deft character sketches, her rather sentimental tableaux, and her enjoyment of ironic contrasts. Sometimes these are no more than the comparisons of California mountain scenes to what she calls "the peaceful apple orchards and smiling river meadows of dear old New England"; at other times they are more fundamental relationships displaying her delight in what she describes as "those scenes just touched with that fine and almost imperceptible *perfume* of the ludicrous." This delight is apparent in her lively little sketches of disparate scenes, persons, and situations. She looks upon the rootless male society from the point of view of a woman who calls herself a "frail, home-loving little thistle," that is a genteel New England lady who nevertheless has plenty of sharp and spiny character. She is amused by male crudities that range from the love of gaudy red calico to the constant profanity of which she writes tolerantly: "Some of these expressions, were they not so fearfully blasphemous, would be grotesquely sublime." She writes amusingly too of the houses men built quickly and sloppily, because they were meant to last no longer than the quickly exhausted mines near which they were constructed; accordingly, she points out, it is common to find the floor "is so uneven that no article of furniture gifted with four legs pretends to stand upon but three at once, so that the chairs, tables, etc., remind you constantly of a dog with a sore foot."

Some comparisons and contrasts, though equally vivid, are more in the Dickensian vein of sentiment, in which contrasting elements are juxtaposed to create an emotional response. Thus she writes of the aftermath of a lynching:

The body of the criminal was allowed to hang for some hours after the execution. It had commenced storming in the early part of the evening; and when those, whose business it was to inter the remains, arrived at the spot they found them enwrapped in a soft, white shroud of feathery snow-flakes, as if pitying Nature had tried to hide from the offended face of heaven, the cruel deed which her mountain children had committed.

Both in attitude and diction, this touching passage anticipates the Dickensian conclusion of Bret Harte's *Outcasts of Poker Flat*:

The wind lulled as if it feared to waken them. Feathery drifts of snow, shaken from the long pine boughs, flew like white-winged birds, and settled about them as they slept. . . . But all human stain, all trace of earthly travail, was hidden beneath the spotless mantle mercifully flung from above. . . . And when pitying fingers brushed the snow from their wan faces, you could scarcely have told from the equal peace that dwelt upon them which was she that had sinned.

Dame Shirley's views anticipated the local color movement of literature in which Bret Harte was to make his reputation, but they were also a development from the attitudes that earlier New Englanders displayed toward California. Tacitly or explicitly New England continues to be used as the criterion by which to measure a new world. Where once the New Englander's basic approach had been to create a contrast between an Anglo-Saxon, Protestant world and a Latin, Catholic one, now the contrast was between the established values and ways of life found at home and those suddenly created in a rough frontier atmosphere by uncultivated pioneers who came from sections of the United States less stable and less sophisticated than New England.

As the gold rush decade of the 1850's faded into the background, New Englanders still continued to come to California, now looking not to make a fortune to take home but to settle down, perhaps permanently, in a new land. Among these later Yankees was Thomas Starr King, a New Yorker by birth but reared in New Hampshire and Massachusetts by New England parents, his father, a Universalist pastor. The son was only twenty-two years old himself when he followed paternal footsteps into the church and was soon presiding over a Unitarian congregation in Boston. But at the age of thirty-six he accepted a call to the people of the Unitarian parish in San Francisco, writing to a friend: "We are unfaithful in huddling so closely around the cosy stove of civilization in this blessed Boston." And so he became another New Englander transplanted to California, yet always aware that Boston was the Hub of the Universe, as Oliver Wendell Holmes put it.

In 1860, the year of his arrival, after settling into his clerical duties King took a vacation trip to the Sierra. This holiday afforded him an opportunity to continue his enthusiastic interest in observing the natural scene that, while in New England, had led to his writing a descriptive book about New Hampshire titled *The White Hills, Their Legends, Landscapes and Poetry*. Like a good one-time Bostonian, King's observations on his California trip were sent to the *Boston Evening Transcript* for issuance in a series of columns. Already established as a writer on nature nearer home, now King, as a very early visitor to Yosemite, brought to New Englanders an acceptable and vivid sense of California's wonders. His so-called "Letters" were lively in their depiction of local characters and graphic in their delineation of the natural scene and both were made more meaningful by an occasional contrast to that which was native to New England. Yet it was the rugged new land that always appealed most to him, so that with great enthusiasm he reported:

The mountains, under the shadow of the evergreens, bloomed with ruby and saffron, with violet and orange. . . . Yet the flowers were obliged to yield in charm to the sugar-pines of that glorious region. I suppose that in three hours we saw ten thousand which were more than two hundred feet high. In the mountain districts of New Hampshire it is very rare to find a hemlock or fir more than three feet in diameter. Time and again we dismounted and put our measuring line around columns, fit to uphold an entablature of Phidias, that were twenty-eight and thirty feet in girth, supporting their topmost spray nearly three hundred feet above us.

King was enchanted by the grand landscape and fascinated by the old Indian associations which endowed the scene with more poetic feeling than it could have evoked were it possessed of but a plain Yankee background.

Is it not delightful, O reader, that the highest cataract in the world bears so noble a name,—Yo-Sem-i-te? It is Indian and signifies "little grizzlies". . . . The valley derives its name from the fact that it abounded once in these majestic beasts. . . . Let the last music that we hear, in turning from the great cataract, be an accompaniment to our gratitude and joy that it keeps the name, "Yo-Sem-i-te".

In the city King looked to New England for cultural standards but in the mountains he was the naturalized Californian who rhapsodically declared: "I do not know what splendors of cascade or sublimities of rock the Himalayas hide; but I would venture something on the faith that nowhere on the globe is there a mile of river scenery that will compare with this Sierra glen, through which the Middle Fork of the Merced makes its two glorious plunges under the shadow of granite walls and soaring pinnacles."

Within three years Thomas Starr King was followed by another New England observer with this same regal surname: Clarence King. They were unrelated by blood but in some ways quite similar in temperament and both were gifted with an ability to describe the natural scene that they enjoyed so enthusiastically. Clarence King was born at Newport, Rhode Island, with a New England heritage stretching back to the *Mayflower*. Graduated from Yale in 1862, he became an unpaid assistant on the geological survey of California conducted by William H. Brewer. There he quickly learned to love the massive mountains of California, Sierra Nevada and Coast Range alike. The grandeur of their granite ridges, their isolated peaks and precipices rising into transparent air and overlooking lower valleys with commanding eminence captivated Clarence King's sense of the sublime. But, mountains aside, King had no use for California. Its "exuberance of grain-field and orchard"; its valleys, "level, fertile, well-watered, half tropically warmed, checkered with . . . ranches of cattle, orchards and vineyard" had, he admitted, "a certain impressive breadth when seen from some overlooking eminence," but when surveyed from nearby they appeared to him to be only "homes of commonplace opulence, towns of bustling thrift," whose very oaks even "seem characterless or gone to sleep when compared with the vitality, the spring, and attitude of the same species higher up on the foot-hills." He admitted that all of this part of California was "a region of great industrial future," but for him it was "quite without charms." Like the valley oaks, "the men and women are dull, unrelieved; they are all alike," King thought, and he was entirely certain as he predicted that "the great

American poet will not book his name from the Sacramento Valley. The people, the acres, the industry seem to be created solely to furnish vulgar fractions in the census."

Clarence King was contemptuous of the California townspeople who lacked a cultural tradition and he was superciliously amused by a family of hunters and pig farmers whom he encountered in the lower Sierra, people he called the Newtys of Pike, a kind of Faulknerian Snopes family of the sort beginning to seep into California's grand mountains. He revealed that the elder Newty's father had actually been a New Englander, but the hog farmer himself was for King a prime example of the melancholy degradation "of beings who have forever lost the conservatism of home and the power of improvement" to such an ultimate degree that King could only believe "that my protoplasm and theirs must be different, in spite of Mr. Huxley."

Although Clarence King was light-hearted and witty in his view of western settlers and did not want to be counted as part "of that saintly army of travellers who write about California, taking pains to open fire (at sublimely long range) with their very hottest shot upon the devoted dwellers here," he was nevertheless a representative New Englander in appreciating the grandeur of California's mountains while looking with scorn and skepticism upon the settlers invading them and all the rest of the land on this farthest western shore. Of these people he declared, "Aspirations for wealth and ease rise conspicuously above any thirst for intellectual culture and moral peace," even though one must recognize that "energy and a glorious audacity are their leading traits." And so King concluded that: "With the gradual decline of gold product, something like social equilibrium asserted itself. By 1860, California had made the vast inspiring stride from barbarism to regularity." He came to believe that Californians might be adding a different sort of species to other

Americans and that perhaps one had to accept them for what they were, rather than comparing them always with representatives of older, more settled societies. Finally, grudgingly, he decided that not only would one have to take them as they were but that one would have to look closely at what that was in itself. So by 1860, only a little more than half a century after the first New Englander visited California, and only a little more than a decade after it had been added as the thirty-first state to the Union, New Englanders, like other Easterners, began to make it their home and thus add their own ways to its amalgam, and began to survey it with more sympathy than they had previously been wont to allow.

There were plenty of New Englanders who continued to come to California during the rest of the 19th century as emigrants, tourists, commentators, romantic interpreters, amateur sociologists, and amused observers. But only a few of these diverse New Englanders wrote books of impressions or interpretations, and fewer yet were of consequence to be remembered. Yet some are still memorable. There was, for example, Helen Hunt Jackson, the daughter of an Amherst professor, against whose unyielding Calvinist dogma she revolted just as she deplored her home town as a "pitiless community" whose "narrowness and monotony," she said, "make rigid the hearts which theology has chilled." Marriage to a westerner changed her environment and made her aware of the plights of other, alien people, most particularly the Indians who had for so long been mistreated by the United States government. To tell their story she wrote a factual but moving book, *A Century of Dishonor*, and then, as an outgrowth of her study of California's Mission Indians, the novel *Ramona*, published in 1884. Intended as the *Uncle Tom's Cabin* of Indian life, it romantically idealized the protection that kindly padres of the missions and fine old Spanish families on California's ranchos ostensibly afforded the Indians and the ways in which white and Indian alike were brutally swept aside by the usurping gringos of the United States. The book became one of America's all-time best sellers as toward the end of the 19th century Americans at last found no danger in a sentimentalized treatment of the Catholic Latin culture they had once scorned and then destroyed.

At just the time that Mrs. Jackson was publishing *Ramona*, another New Englander, Charles Fletcher Lummis, was turning his eyes toward California. A young Massachusetts man, just two years past his A.B. at Harvard, Lummis came to California in the dramatically unorthodox style that characterized everything he did. He took 143 days of 1884 and 1885 to walk west from Ohio to Los Angeles, in a journey which he described for the *Los Angeles Times*, whose city editor he became soon after arrival. An emotional and flamboyant man, Lummis fell passionately in love with the Pacific Southwest whose Spanish culture and Indian past he studied seriously and popularized enthusiastically. He founded and edited a promotional magazine whose original title, *Land of Sunshine*, was later changed to the somewhat less booster-like *Out West*. Under both mastheads it gave him a forum for his articles and those he commissioned on such favorite topics as Spanish culture, the California way of life, Southwestern history, preservation and conservation of the natural scene, the lore of the past Indian, and improved treatment of the modern Indian. For its pages he got contributions from Joaquin Miller, Jack London, Frank Norris, and Robinson Jeffers, among many others. He founded a museum in Los Angeles to collect anthropological materials of the Southwest, he created the Landmarks Club to restore the missions and to preserve other historic buildings, he established an important collection of Southwestern books and manuscripts in the Los Angeles Public Library of which he was head for five years, he wrote numerous books to promote his ideas and his adopted region, and he built with his own hands a home in the Southwestern regional style of architecture that became a center for all people sympathetic to his views. All this occasioned President Theodore Roosevelt, his friend since Harvard days, to say: "The West owes you a lot," to which Lummis not surprisingly replied, "What? Why, I owe everything to the West. It *made* me. I found myself there!"

Toward the end of the 19th century California had obviously become for some New Englanders not only a sunny haven from a cold climate but even more a release from a culture they considered glacial and stultifying. The original theological force of Calvinism now having dwindled to what they thought of as but a mean and mundane morality, these great-grandsons of the Puritans looked for an escape by traveling to the opposite coast of the United States, as far away as possible from home and all it stood for. Among such emigrants from the citadel of New England was Gelett Burgess. He too was a rebel, like Helen Hunt Jackson and Charles Fletcher Lummis, against an ancestral culture, but he possessed his own temperament and tastes, very different from theirs and productive of a very different artistic expression.

Burgess, who had been reared in Boston, was conscious of a two-hundred-year-old heritage of Puritan religion and sober gentility inculcated by a very proper family. He left this established world to come to San Francisco in the 1880's, an engineer fresh out of M.I.T. who had been employed as an instructor of mechanical drawing at the University of California in Berkeley. The greater city of San Francisco across the Bay attracted him immediately for it offered as contrast to his staid hometown a bizare, variegated, and cosmopolitan atmosphere permeated by what was called the spirit of the fin de siècle. It was a city in which, he said, "Tuesday becomes Thursday with scarcely time for a Wednesday between, where every language under the moon is spoken, and every street climbs a half-dozen hills, changing its character at every lamppost." Gelett Burgess never saw a purple cow but it was in San Francisco that he conjured up the thought of the fantastic beast with which his name has ever since been associated. To Burgess it was only in San Francisco that such wild conceits could be created and published in the days known by the more placid color of the mauve decade. This city was so romantic for him that of it he wrote a delightful local color novel titled *The Heart Line,* and he exuberantly espoused the high jinks of the city's bohemianism in ways that led to his ousting from the university and his giving up of engineering and mechanical drawing for the freely penned fantasy of his boneless quasi-human Goops. San Francisco was for him "the mistress of five hundred miles of coastline, the outlet of a hundred fertile valleys," and California he declared, "is, to all purposes of communication, an island . . . here are no old gods set round with formulae and dogma. Here one may stay young till the end."

And so California, old (that is, Spanish and Mexican) and new (that is, post–Gold Rush frontier) finally came to be seen by the diverse New Englanders as strange, romantic, and attractive. It was, as Carey McWilliams called it, "the great exception" in the vast American expanse of uniformity. Once contemptible because it was different, in the 20th century it became desirable for this very reason. The fascination that California exerted came to make it the most populous state in the Union and an amalgam of culture as definite in its ways as that of New England, on the nation's opposite coast. Over the years as it manifested its own character, both the scene and the civilization of California, in the proverbial expression, had been entered now in the bad books, now in the good books of New Englanders, who variously viewed it unfavorably and favorably. Finally, visitors and emigrants alike, New Englanders and others came to terms with California by accepting it in itself and for what it offered. So in a handfull of books (perhaps not enough to form a respectable bibliography), all written within sixty years by a few persons from one region about another, one may find documentation for a small but special sort of cultural history.